About This Book

With the birth of human speech came the birth of stories and song. The resulting rich cultural heritage includes myths, legends, epic poems, Bible stories, fairy tales, lullabies, folk songs—and religious songs of praise, or hymns.

Hymns are simple, memorable songs that people like to sing, that have offered comfort in times of great pain and stress, that have expressed gratitude, joy, and hope. They are life-affirming messages that convey moral values and unite people in prayer and faith. They reveal, in plain language, powerful truths about the human condition, inspiring musicians, artists, and writers as diverse as Emily Dickinson, T. S. Eliot, and Garrison Keillor.

Replacing the chanting of psalms, hymns were first widely sung in the eighteenth century. The earliest hymns were Christmas carols and Easter songs. Now there are an estimated five million hymns in over two hundred languages.

The fifteen hymns in this book are songs that continue to be popular and speak meaningfully to the mysteries of contemporary life. They have stood the test of time to become classic songs of praise.

This book grew out of the eight years I was an organist at St. Joseph's Church in Wilmette, Illinois. It always fascinated me that centuries-old tunes could make people feel good—cheered and uplifted—while also serving as a valuable part of that day's service. The music seemed to cut across boundaries of age, nationality, sex, financial status, and politics to unite the congregation in a swell of universal emotion. And it appeared to me that people were having fun.

It is my hope that this book will extend the joyful singing of hymns outward from church, particularly to homes, where I hope it will be inspirational to parents and children.

—Kathleen Krull
San Diego, California

I wanted the artwork to reflect the grandeur of the hymns as well as their beautiful simplicity. The illustrations are based on several versions of the Book of Hours, a type of decorated prayer book used in the late Middle Ages by the nobility as well as the common people. This book, like the Book of Hours, follows the seasons and labors of the year beginning with early spring and ending with winter.

—Kathryn Hewitt
Santa Monica, California

D1172192

SONGS of PRAISE

Collected and Arranged by

Kathleen Krull

Illustrated by

Kathryn Hewitt

Harcourt Brace Jovanovich, Publishers • San Diego New York London

HBJ

Text and musical arrangements
copyright © 1988 by Kathleen Krull
Illustrations copyright © 1988 by Kathryn Hewitt

All rights reserved. No part of this publication
may be reproduced or transmitted in any form
or by any means, electronic or mechanical, including photocopy,
recording, or any information storage and retrieval system,
without permission in writing from the publisher.

Requests for permission to make copies of any part
of the work should be mailed to:
Permissions, Harcourt Brace Jovanovich, Publishers,
Orlando, Florida 32887.

Library of Congress Cataloging-in-Publication Data
Songs of praise.
Fifteen hymns with notes and extra verses
printed as text with each work.
Summary: A collection of fifteen classic hymns, each
with a historical note and piano accompaniment.
1. Hymns, English. [1. Hymns] I. Krull, Kathleen.
II. Hewitt, Kathryn, ill.
M2193.S6965   1988   87-751091
ISBN 0-15-277108-5
Printed in the United States of America
First edition
A B C D E

The paintings in this book were done in watercolor
and gouache on 90 lb. d'Arches hot-press paper.
Music and text composition by A-R Editions, Madison, Wisconsin
The display type was set in Centaur and the text type was set in Palatino.
Color separations were made by Heinz Weber, Inc., Los Angeles, California.
Printed by Holyoke Lithograph, Springfield, Massachusetts
Bound by The Book Press, Inc., Brattleboro, Vermont
Production supervision by Rebecca Miller and Warren Wallerstein
Designed by Camilla Filancia

A - men.

To my parents
    —Kathleen Krull

To Oma Reeves, with love
    —Kathryn Hewitt

CENTRAL ARKANSAS LIBRARY SYSTEM
LITTLE ROCK PUBLIC LIBRARY
700 LOUISIANA STREET
LITTLE ROCK, ARKANSAS 72201

Faith of Our Fathers

The idea that faith is strong enough to withstand all of life's trials has made this an enduring, comforting song. The sincere lyrics by Father Faber (1814–1863) were not set to Englishman Henri Hemy's (1818–1888) music until after Faber's death.

Frederick Faber

Henri Hemy

Faith of our fa - thers, liv - ing still In spite of dun-geon, fire, and sword!

2. Faith of our fathers, God's great power
Shall win all nations unto thee;
And through the truth that comes from God
Mankind shall then indeed be free. *Chorus.*

3. Faith of our fathers, we will love
Both friend and foe in all our strife,
And preach thee, too, as love knows how,
By kindly words and virtuous life. *Chorus.*

Christ the Lord Is Risen Today

This beautiful Easter melody is from "Lyra Davidica," an anonymous collection of songs published in 1708. Charles Wesley (1707–1788) is credited with writing the words to more than 6,500 hymns. Shouting "Alleluia!" on Easter morning was an old Christian custom.

2. Lives again our glorious King: Alleluia!
   Where, O death, is now thy sting? Alleluia!
   Once he died our souls to save: Alleluia!
   Where's thy victory, boasting grave? Alleluia!

Amazing Grace

John Newton (1725–1807) had been a slave-owner before he changed his life and became a clergyman. Thankful for the ability to recognize that his life had been immoral, he wrote this song. Millions of people have sung it since, cherishing the hope it offers for change and growth.

John Newton
American folk melody

Sweetly

A - maz - ing _ grace! How sweet the sound That saved a _ wretch like me! _____

I once — was — lost, but now — am — found, Was blind, but — now I see. ——

2. 'Twas grace that taught my heart to fear,
   And grace my fears relieved;
   How precious did that grace appear
   The hour I first believed!

3. Through many dangers, toils, and snares
   I have already come;
   'Tis grace that brought me safe thus far,
   And grace will lead me home.

Joyful, Joyful, We Adore Thee

The triumphant conclusion to the Ninth Symphony of Beethoven (1770–1827) is a series of choral variations on this majestic melody. Beethoven used the words to Schiller's poem "Ode to Joy," an affirmation of the value of life and the ordinary human being. Several hymns have since used this melody. The version here is by Henry van Dyke (1852–1933), who was inspired to write it after viewing the Berkshire Mountains in England.

Henry van Dyke   Ludwig van Beethoven

Joy-ful, joy-ful,   we a-dore Thee, God of glo-ry,   Lord of love; Hearts un-fold like flowers be-fore Thee,

2. All Thy works with joy surround Thee,
Earth and heaven reflect Thy rays,
Stars and angels sing around Thee,
Center of unbroken praise.

Field and forest, vale and mountain,
Flowery meadow, flashing sea,
Chanting bird and flowing fountain,
Call us to rejoice in Thee.

Blest Be the Tie That Binds

This sweet melody is by Johann Naegeli (1768–1836), director of the Swiss Association for the Cultivation of Music. John Fawcett (1740–1817) was a Baptist minister who was tempted to take a higher-paying job. When his congregation gathered around him to show their appreciation, he was touched and decided to stay. He wrote these words in praise of the love that binds people together.

John Fawcett

Johann Naegeli

Blest be ___ the tie ___ that binds Our hearts _ in Chris - tian love;

The fel - low - ship _ of kin - dred minds _ Is like _ to that _ a - bove.

2. Before our Father's throne
   We pour our ardent prayers;
   Our fears, our hopes, our aims are one,
   Our comforts and our cares.

3. We share each other's woes,
   Each other's burdens bear;
   And often for each other flows
   The sympathizing tear.

Jesus Loves Me!

Simple words and a charming tune make this a Sunday School favorite. For many years, Anna Warner (1820–1915) conducted a Bible class for the cadets of the United States Military Academy at West Point. William Bradbury (1816–1868) was an American composer and music editor.

Anna Warner

William Bradbury

Sweetly

Je - sus loves me! This I know, For the Bi - ble tells me so; Lit - tle ones to

2. Jesus loves me! He who died,
   Heaven's gate to open wide;
   He will wash away my sin,
   Let His little child come in. *Chorus.*

3. Jesus, take this heart of mine,
   Make it pure and wholly Thine;
   On the cross You died for me;
   I will try to live for Thee. *Chorus.*

Nearer, My God, to Thee

Sarah Adams (1805–1848) based this plea for a closer relationship with God on the Biblical story of Jacob's dream. About the melody, Lowell Mason (1792–1872) said: "One night some time after lying awake in the dark, eyes wide open, through the stillness of the house the melody came to me, and the next morning I wrote down the notes." It is said that this hymn was played by the ship's band as the oceanliner *Titanic* was sinking on April 14, 1912.

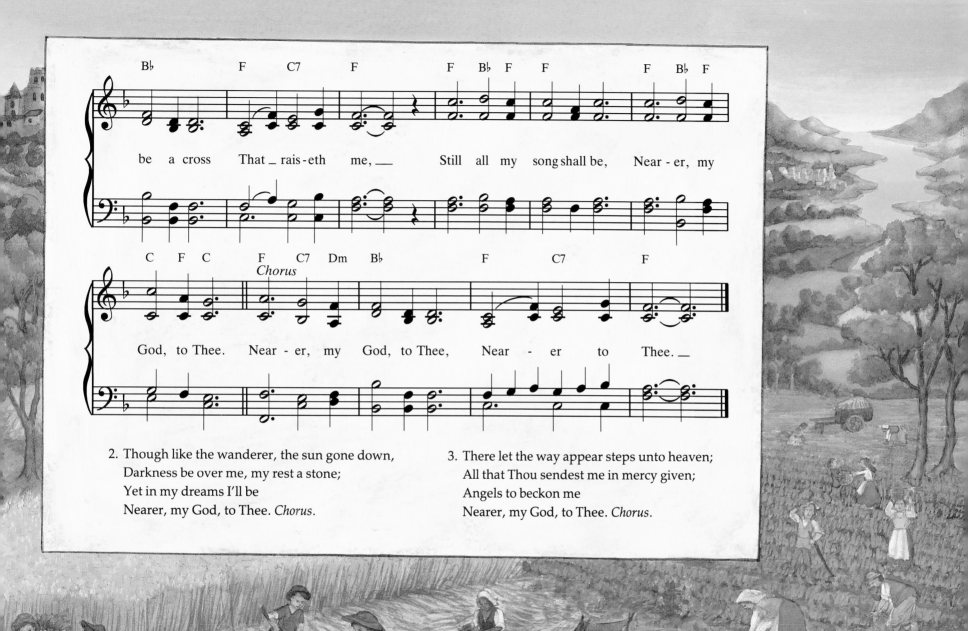

2. Though like the wanderer, the sun gone down,
   Darkness be over me, my rest a stone;
   Yet in my dreams I'll be
   Nearer, my God, to Thee. *Chorus.*

3. There let the way appear steps unto heaven;
   All that Thou sendest me in mercy given;
   Angels to beckon me
   Nearer, my God, to Thee. *Chorus.*

God of Our Fathers

Daniel Roberts (1841–1907), a country parson, wrote the words to this rousing prayer of praise for the 1876 Fourth of July celebration in Brandon, Vermont. His words were first combined with this melody, written by George Warren (1828–1876), at a service at St. Thomas's Church in New York City in 1892. This hymn is often accompanied by trumpets.

Daniel Roberts

George Warren

With a flourish

God of our fa-thers, whose al-might-y hand Leads forth in beau-ty all the star-ry band

Of shin-ing worlds in splen-dor through the skies, Our grate-ful songs be-fore Thy throne a-rise.

2. Thy love divine hath led us in the past;
In this free land by Thee our lot is cast;

Be Thou our ruler, guardian, guide, and stay,
Thy word our law, Thy paths our chosen way.

Praise God, from Whom All Blessings Flow

The first verse, by Bishop Ken (1637–1711), is considered to be the most famous doxology, or expression of praise used in church. The second verse, based on Psalm 100, is by Scotsman William Kethe (about 1530–1608) and is interchangeable with the first. This is thought to be one of the few hymns Shakespeare knew.

Thomas Ken *(first verse)* and William Kethe *(second verse)*   Louis Bourgeois

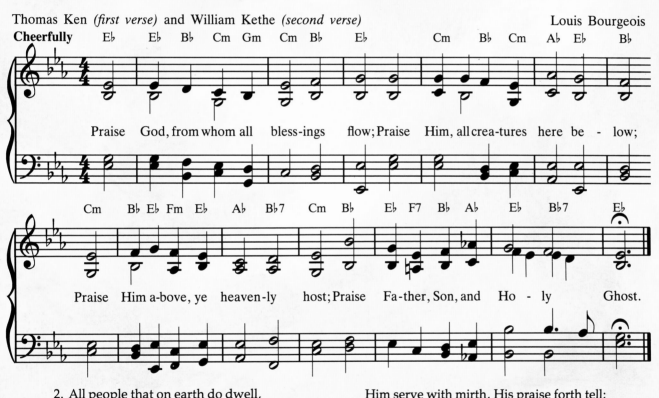

Praise God, from whom all bless-ings flow; Praise Him, all crea-tures here be - low;

Praise Him a-bove, ye heaven-ly host; Praise Fa-ther, Son, and Ho - ly Ghost.

2. All people that on earth do dwell,   Him serve with mirth, His praise forth tell;
   Sing to the Lord with cheerful voice;   Come ye before Him and rejoice.

A Mighty Fortress Is Our God

This classic hymn is based on Psalm 46 and was first published in 1529. It became the battle song of Protestants persecuted at the time, many of whom died as martyrs. An eloquent testament to courage in the face of conflict and temptation, it has served as a battle song since. In 1942, for example, Norwegians sang it as they defied a Nazi order to close the ancient Trondheim Cathedral.

WORDS AND MUSIC: Martin Luther, English translation by Frederick Hedge

A might-y for-tress is __ our God, A bul-wark nev-er fail - ing.
Our help-er He __ a - mid __ the flood Of mor-tal ills pre - vail - ing.

2. Did we in our own strength confide,   The man of God's own choosing.   Lord Sabaoth His name,
Our striving would be losing,   Dost ask who that may be?   From age to age the same,
Were not the right man on our side,   Christ Jesus, it is He—   And He must win the battle.

Now Thank We All Our God

This song is all the more powerful for having been written during a time of war and plague, when Pastor Rinkart (1586–1649) buried almost 4,500 plague victims, among them his wife. With lyrics based on Ecclesiasticus 1:22–24, the hymn is often sung at ceremonies celebrating the end of a war or the completion of a cathedral.

Martin Rinkart, translated by Catherine Winkworth

Johann Crüger

Enthusiastically

Now thank we all our God With hearts and hands and voic - es,
Who won-drous things hath done, In whom His world re - joic - es;

2. Oh, may this bounteous God through all our life be near us,
   With ever joyful hearts and blessed peace to cheer us;
   And keep us in His Grace, and guide us when perplexed,
   And free us from all ills in this world and the next.

O God, Our Help in Ages Past

This hymn's universality makes it a frequent choice for funerals and major events. It was played on British radio, for example, on September 3, 1939, the day World War II was declared. Based on Psalm 90, the words were written by Isaac Watts (1674–1748), who wrote more than 600 hymns, including many for children. The melody is by William Croft (1678–1727), a distinguished English composer of church music.

Isaac Watts
In a spirit of grandeur

William Croft

O God, our help in a-ges past, Our hope for years to come,

Our shel-ter from the storm-y blast, And our e-ter-nal home.

2. Under the shadow of Thy throne
   Still may we dwell secure;
   Sufficient is Thine arm alone,
   And our defense is sure.

3. A thousand ages in Thy sight
   Are like an evening gone;
   Short as the watch that ends the night
   Before the rising sun.

We Gather Together

After his country's liberation from Spain, an unknown Netherlander wrote this hymn, first published in 1626, expressing gratitude. The simple words of thanks and praise are universal and timeless; many Americans find them especially appealing at Thanksgiving.

Author unknown, English translation by Theodore Baker

Traditional Netherlands melody

Soothingly

We gath - er to - geth - er to ask the Lord's bless - ing; He chas - tens and

2. Beside us to guide us, our God with us joining,
   Ordaining, maintaining His kingdom divine;

   So from the beginning the fight we were winning:
   Thou, Lord, was at our side—all glory be Thine.

Holy, Holy, Holy

Bishop Heber (1783–1826) composed these words to celebrate the Holy Trinity—Father, Son, and Holy Ghost. A year after Heber's death, the song was finally published. Later, the lively musical setting by John Dykes (1823–1876) immediately made this hymn the favorite of many people, including the English poet Tennyson, who arranged for it to be sung at his funeral.

Reginald Heber

John Dykes

Majestic

Ho - ly, ho - ly, ho - ly, Lord God Al - might - y! Ear - ly in the

2. Holy, holy, holy, all the saints adore Thee,
   Casting down their golden crowns around the glassy sea;

Cherubim and seraphim falling down before Thee,
Who wert, and art, and evermore shalt be.

Rock of Ages

According to legend, this famous hymn was written after Augustus Toplady (1740–1778) found refuge during a thunderstorm in the cleft, or opening, of a rock. In this stirring song, the rock becomes Jesus, the storm becomes sin, and the need for refuge becomes a plea for salvation.

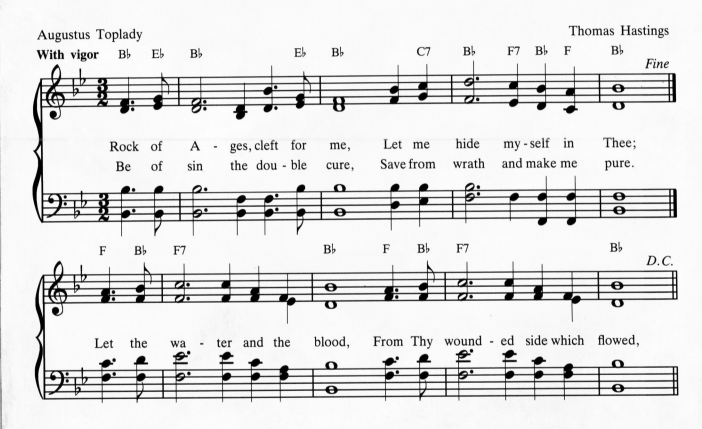

2. While I draw this final breath, when my eyes shall close in death,
   When I rise to worlds unknown, and behold Thee on Thy throne,
   Rock of Ages, cleft for me, let me hide myself in Thee.